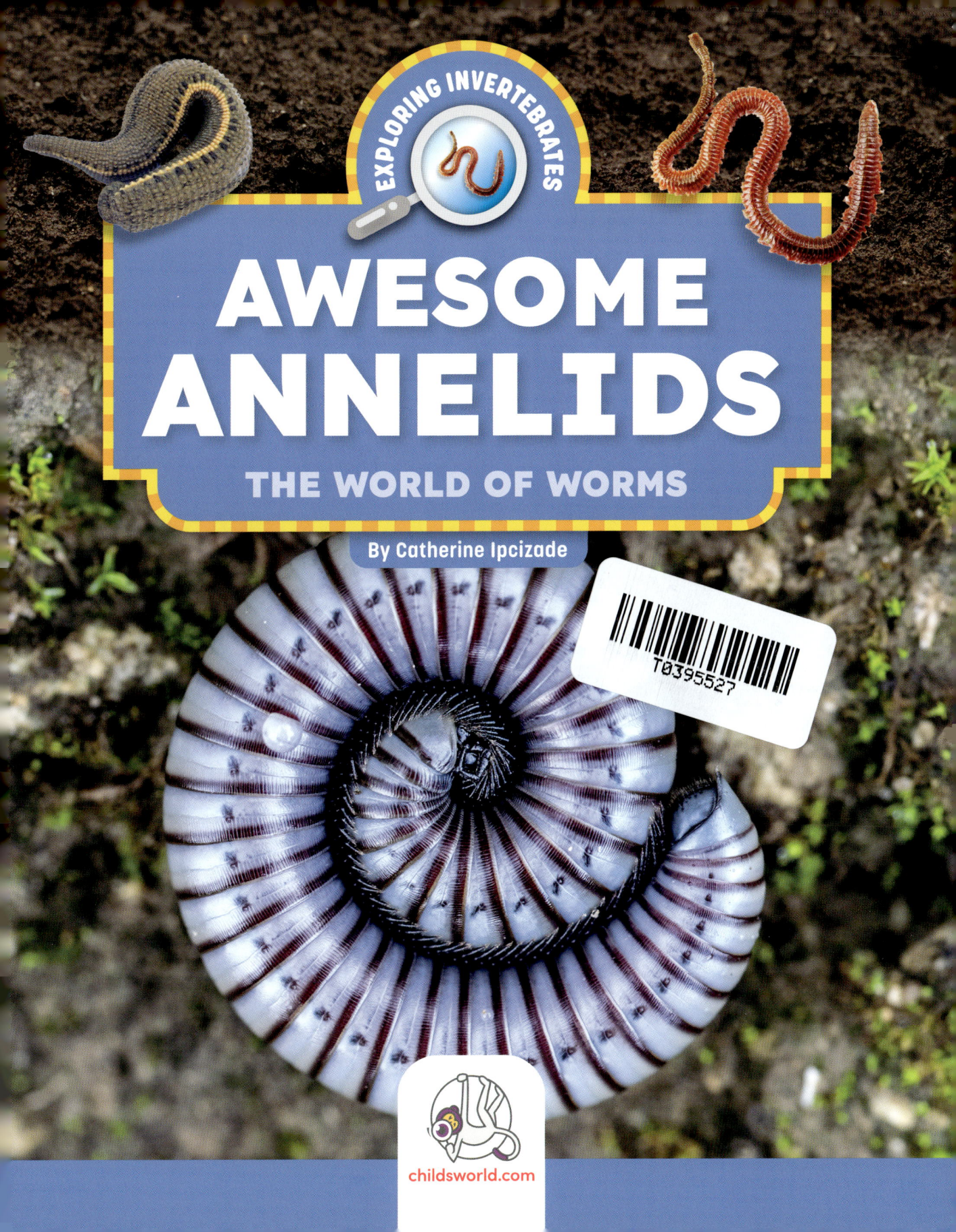

EXPLORING INVERTEBRATES

AWESOME ANNELIDS

THE WORLD OF WORMS

By Catherine Ipcizade

The Child's World
childsworld.com

Published by The Child's World®
800-599-READ • childsworld.com

Photography Credits
Cover: ©Jose A. Bernat Bacete/Getty Images; ©Yutthasart Yanakomsiri/Shutterstock; ©Nenov/Getty Images; page 5: ©279photo Studio/Shutterstock; ©Richard Peterson/Shutterstock; ©Ajay Tvm/Shutterstock; ©Anton Peichev/Shutterstock; ©Rattiya Thongdumhyu/Shutterstock; ©timsimages.uk/Shutterstock; page 6: ©Humberto Ramirez/Getty Images; page 8: ©Stuart Westmorland/Getty Images; page 9: ©279photo Studio/Shutterstock; ©schankz/Shutterstock; page 10: ©Antagain/Getty Images; ©Darwin Fan/Getty Images; page 11: ©Nataly Studio/Shutterstock; page 13: ©Gerald Robert Fischer/Shutterstock; ©AZ 54design/Shutterstock; page 15: ©Pandu Saputro/Getty Images; ©Oleh Strus/Getty Images; page 16: ©Iuliia Petrovskaia/Getty Images; ©page 18: ©Glenn Cantor/Getty Images; page 19: ©Ed Reschke/Getty Images; page 22: ©Lori Bye

ISBN Information
9781503894518 (Reinforced Library Binding)
9781503894808 (Portable Document Format)
9781503895621 (Online Multi-user eBook)
9781503896444 (Electronic Publication)

LCCN
2024942888

Printed in the United States of America

ABOUT THE AUTHOR
Catherine Ipcizade is a college professor and the author of more than 30 books for children. She loves photography, cooking, and spending time with her family in sunny California and the mountains of Utah. Her favorite word is "serendipity" because life is full of unexpected, fortunate surprises.

CONTENTS

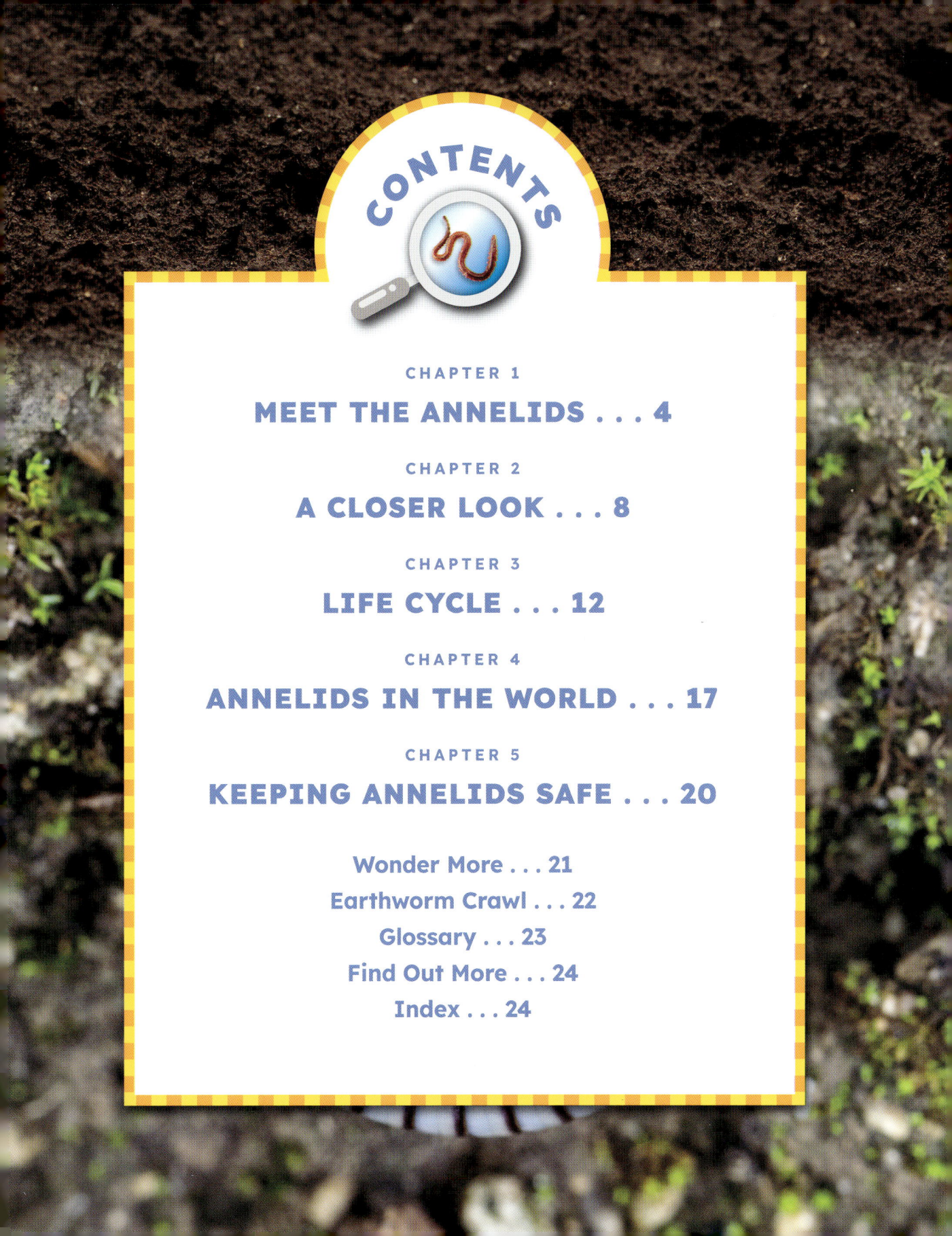

CHAPTER 1

MEET THE ANNELIDS

It has just rained. The ground is damp. An earthworm wiggles its way through the soil. The worm is part of a large group of animals called annelids. Annelids are part of the largest group of animals, the **invertebrates**. Annelids include worms and leeches.

There are more than 15,000 **species** of annelids. They come in many shapes and sizes. The tiniest annelids are nearly invisible! The largest annelids are giant earthworms. The giant Gippsland earthworm and the Mekong giant earthworm can both reach up to 9 feet (2.7 meters) in length. That's longer than most snakes!

SOME AWESOME ANNELIDS

leech

earthworm

millipede

clam worm

sandworm

Annelids eat different things. Leeches feed on blood. Earthworms feed on dead plants and animals within the soil. They are **decomposers**. **Polychaete** (POL-ee-keet) worms may eat dead matter on the ocean floor. They also eat other worms and sometimes use **gills** to suck in tiny creatures from the water. Some polychaete worms even live inside other creatures, such as clams. These worms eat by absorbing some of the food particles the other creatures eat.

For annelids, home might be on the land or in the water. They live all over the world. There are annelids in the deep ocean. There are annelids in the forests. Lakes, ponds, and streams are where leeches are most often found. Earthworms love damp soil. They are often found burrowing in backyards, gardens, and forests. Polychaete worms enjoy the ocean floor. They are called **bottom-dwellers**.

NO SWIMMERS HERE!

Even though most leeches live in fresh water such as lakes, not all types of leeches are strong swimmers! They often live in slow-moving or still water. That helps leeches to hide until a **host** comes by. A common host might be a fish, a frog, or even a turtle. Once the leech latches on, the host does the swimming.

Polychaete worms appear fuzzy, but don't touch one—their bristles sting if they are handled.

CHAPTER 2

A CLOSER LOOK

The three most common annelids are earthworms, polychaete worms, and leeches. They are different creatures, but they have one thing in common— they all have segmented bodies. That means their body is made up of sections. Annelids move like accordions. That's because they have two sets of muscles. They stretch each section of their bodies, and then they squeeze them shut again. One set of muscles helps with stretching. Another set of muscles helps with squeezing. This makes annelids unique. Other invertebrates do not have segmented bodies.

LET'S TAKE A LOOK!

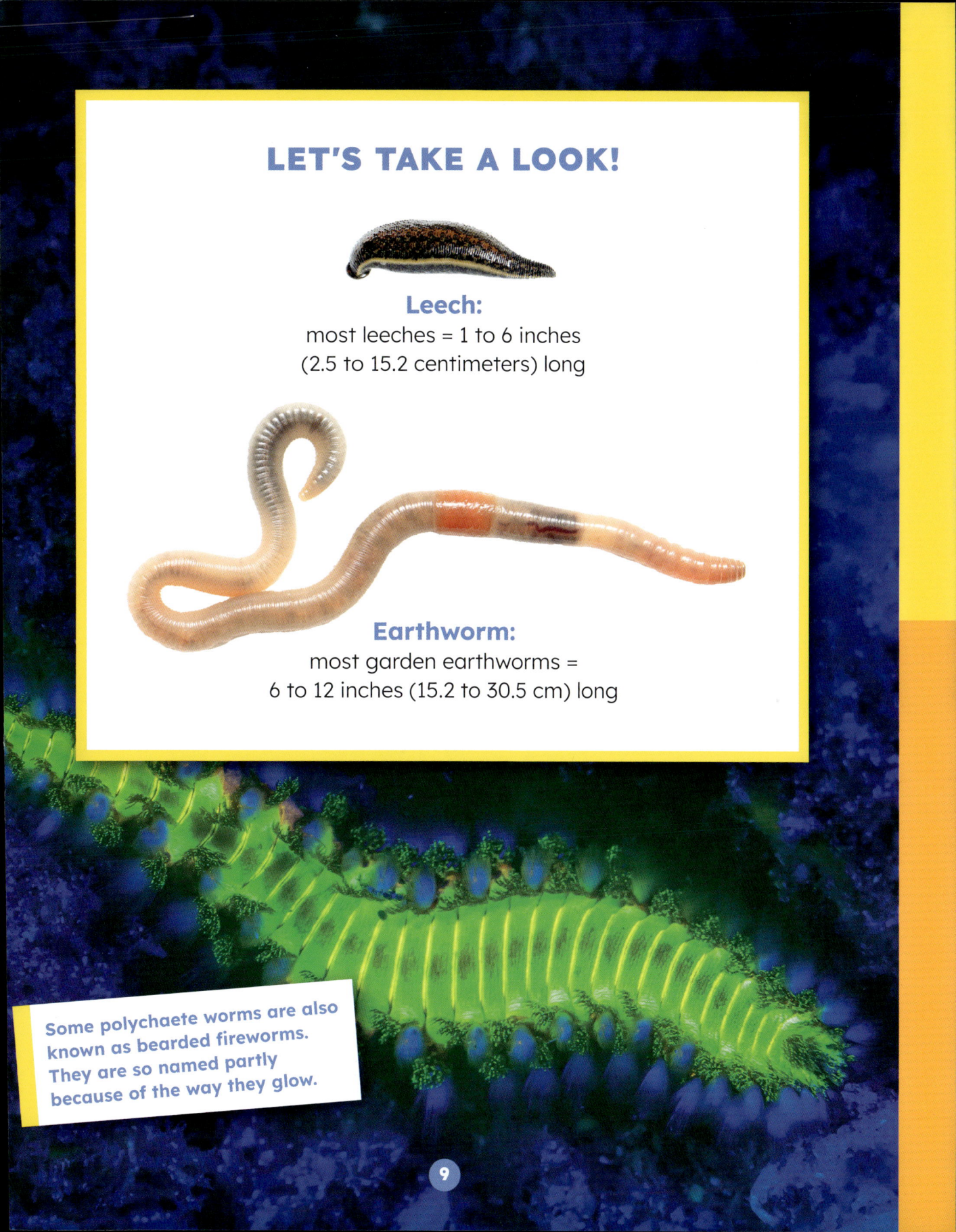

Leech:
most leeches = 1 to 6 inches
(2.5 to 15.2 centimeters) long

Earthworm:
most garden earthworms =
6 to 12 inches (15.2 to 30.5 cm) long

Some polychaete worms are also known as bearded fireworms. They are so named partly because of the way they glow.

LEECHES— A MEDICAL MARVEL?

Leeches used to be very important in the medical world. When a person had an infection, a doctor placed a leech on them. The leech sucked out extra blood and helped heal the infection. Today, modern medicine has mostly replaced the need to use leeches in medical practice.

Many birds eat earthworms, but robins eat the most. A single robin eats up to 14 feet (427 centimeters) of earthworms a day.

When a scale worm senses danger, its spots light up. The **predator** goes away. Polychaete worms, such as scale worms, sometimes glow. The scale worm has colorful scales that glow in different colors! This glowing is called **bioluminescence**. It helps the worms to communicate. It scares away predators. It attracts **prey**, too.

A robin pulls an earthworm from the soil and gulps it down. It eats the worm to survive. Earthworms are prey for many creatures. When an earthworm burrows into the soil, it's not playing hide-and-seek. All that feeding on dead leaves and animal matter makes the soil healthy. So does the act of wriggling through the dirt. That helps loosen up the soil so new plants can grow. Earthworms are superheroes in the annelid world.

CHAPTER 3

LIFE CYCLE

Earthworms have a raised band of skin, called a saddle, about halfway down their bodies. When an earthworm is ready to have babies, a layer of slime forms around the saddle. The worm slides out of the slime, which becomes a **cocoon**. There are between one and 20 eggs inside. The baby worms grow inside the cocoon for two to three weeks, and then they are born.

Leeches are a bit different. They lay a sack of eggs and soon, new leeches are born. Some polychaete worms lay cocoons and some grow baby worms inside their bodies. Some worms grow a small bud on their bodies. That bud forms a whole new worm. This is called "**budding**."

EARTHWORM LIFE CYCLE

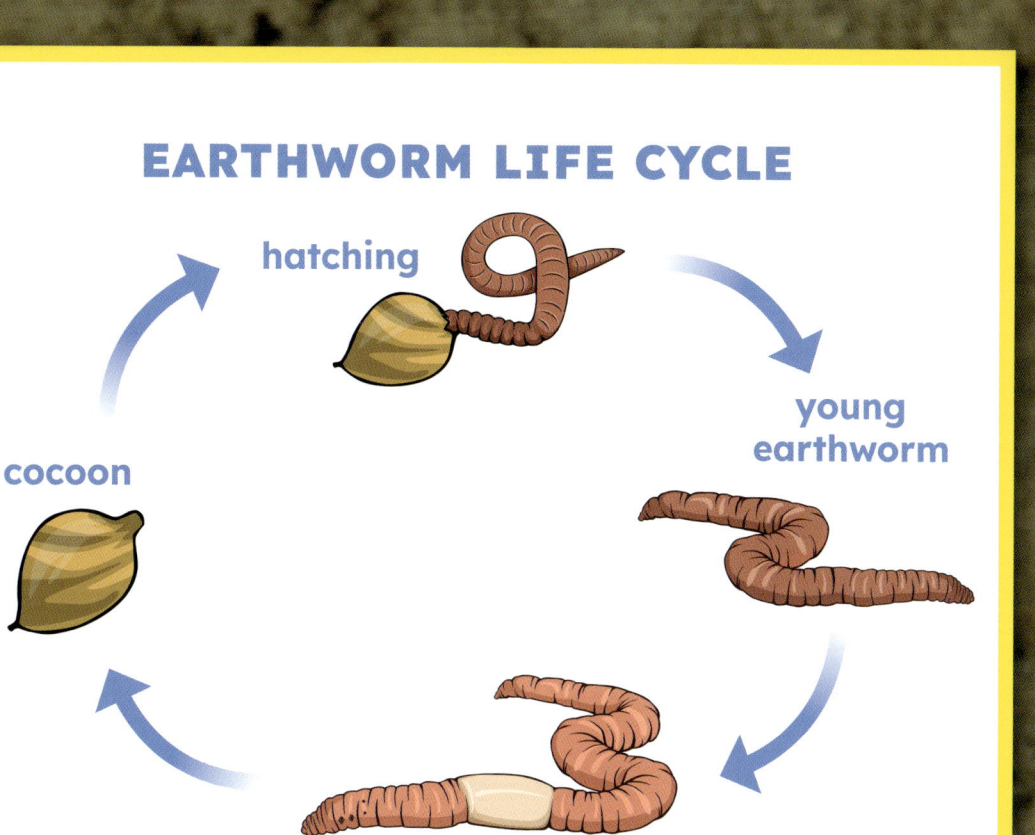

hatching

young earthworm

adult earthworm

cocoon

Bobbit worms can grow up to 10 feet (305 cm) long. They can snap their prey in half, and stings from their spines cause numbness in humans.

Like many creatures, each annelid species has a different lifespan. That means not all annelid species live for the same number of years. Some annelids live much longer than others. Worms and other annelids that are common prey might have a shorter life. Most earthworms live two to eight years. That's a long time for an invertebrate.

Polychaete worms usually live about one to two years. It's not easy living on the ocean floor. Food can be scarce there. It can also be dark. Leeches rely on bloodsucking to live, so they often survive anywhere from one to 10 years.

Millipedes have up to 100 segments. Each segment has two sets of legs attached.

When earthworms mate, each worm produces a cocoon that contains baby worms.

Bloodworms are often used as bait because most fish eat them.

ANNELIDS IN THE WORLD

Annelids live alone. They do not need each other to hunt or find shelter. They wiggle and burrow into small spaces for shelter or to hide. But annelids are important to the food chain. There are many annelids in the world. Polychaete worms make up the largest group. They are called bottom-dwellers because many of them rest on the ocean floor. This makes them an important part of the food chain because they keep the oceans clean.

Bloodworms are important for the food chain, too. They live in shallow waters and like to burrow in wet mud. Bloodworms are a favorite food for fish. Without enough bloodworms as a food source, fish would die. That would hurt the food chain. Animals that eat fish would then not have enough food to survive. Fishermen use bloodworms as bait. This helps them catch fish that can be fed to humans or other animals.

Annelids help the environment every day. As decomposers, earthworms help the soil and plants so new crops can grow. When polychaete worms eat dead matter on the ocean floor, they are cleaning it up. That keeps the water safe so other species can thrive. Leeches can be both helpful and harmful. Some contribute to disease in other animals when they suck their blood. But many leeches feed on creatures that can hurt the environment.

Although both ends look the same, earthworms have a head and a tail. An earthworm's head is the end of its body closest to the saddle.

KEEPING ANNELIDS SAFE

When people **compost** food, earthworms have nutritious food to eat. They help keep the soil healthy so new plants can grow. Polychaete worms and leeches also rely on humans to make good choices. When humans are careful to keep water sources clean, it helps polychaete worms and leeches survive longer.

Annelids are interesting to observe, but it is best to leave them where we find them. They have an important job to do each day. They rely on humans to be mindful of keeping the planet clean. This will help ensure that annelids will continue to thrive on Earth.

WONDER MORE

Wondering About New Information

What new information did you learn about annelids from this book? What surprised you? Write down two of the most surprising facts.

Wondering How It Matters

Earthworms burrow into soil. Why is this important? What would happen to plants if worms did not burrow in the soil?

Wondering Why

Why do you think leeches aren't often used in medicine anymore?

Ways to Keep Wondering

After reading this book, what questions do you have about annelids? Which annelids would you like to learn more about? What can you do to learn more about them?

EARTHWORM CRAWL

Earthworms burrow in the dirt. They eat decaying plants along the way. This keeps our soil healthy. For this activity, you'll create your own earthworm habitat. Unlike real earthworm habitats, this is one you can eat!

Steps to Take

1. Put sandwich cookies into a plastic bag. Use a rolling pin to crush the cookies.

2. Pour the crushed cookies into the cup.

3. Tear up a few mint leaves into tiny pieces.

4. Nestle the gummy worms and mint leaves in the cup to look like worms burrowing in the dirt.

5. Dig in!

Supplies

- clear plastic cup
- brown sandwich cookies
- gummy worms
- fresh mint, lettuce, or some other leafy herb or vegetable

GLOSSARY

bioluminescence (by-oh-loom-uh-NESS-ents) Bioluminescence is what happens when an animal makes chemicals that cause its body to glow.

bottom-dwellers (BAH-tum DWELL-urs) Bottom-dwellers are creatures that live at the bottom of the ocean floor.

budding (BUD-ing) Budding happens when a worm grows a bud on its body that then becomes a new worm.

cocoon (kuh-KOON) A cocoon is a covering or case made by some animals that protects them as they grow.

compost (KOM-post) Composting is the process of using leftover food as fertilizer for the land.

decomposers (dee-kom-POE-zurz) Decomposers are creatures that break down dead organisms in soil or water into smaller particles.

host (HOST) A host is a living plant or animal that a parasite lives in or on.

invertebrates (in-VER-tuh-bruts) Invertebrates are animals that do not have a backbone.

molt (MOHLT) When an invertebrate molts, it sheds its hard exoskeleton in order to grow bigger.

polychaete (POL-ee-keet) A polychaete is a type of worm that lives in the water.

predator (PRED-uh-tur) A predator is an animal that hunts other animals for food.

prey (PRAY) Prey is an animal that is hunted for food.

species (SPEE-shees) A species is a group of living things that can reproduce.

FIND OUT MORE

In the Library

French, Vivian. *Yucky Worms*. Somerville, MA: Candlewick Press, 2021.

Glaser, Linda. *Wonderful Worms*. Minneapolis, MN: Millbrook Press, 2021.

Percival, Kari. *How to Say Hello to a Worm*. New York, NY: Penguin, 2022.

Tordjman, Nathalie. *The Book of Tiny Creatures*. San Francisco, CA: Chronicle Books, 2021.

On the Web

Visit our website for links about annelids: **childsworld.com/links**

Note to Parents, Caregivers, Teachers, and Librarians: We routinely verify our web links to make sure they are safe and active sites. So encourage your readers to check them out!

INDEX